Down on the Farm

COWS

Hannah Ray

QED Publishing

QED

First published in the UK in 2006 by
QED Publishing
A Quarto Group company
226 City Road
London ECIV 2TT
www.qed-publishing.co.uk

A Catalogue record for this book is available
from the British Library.

ISBN 1 84538 355 9

Written by Hannah Ray
Designed by Liz Wiffen
Consultant Sally Morgan
Editor Paul Manning
Picture Researcher Joanne Forrest Smith
Illustrations by Chris Davidson

Publisher Steve Evans
Editorial Director Jean Coppendale
Art Director Zeta Davies

Printed and bound in China

Picture credits

Key: t = top, b = bottom, c = centre,
l = left, r = right, FC = front cover

Alamy Peter Dean 7, /David R Frazier Photolibrary.Inc.
13, /Lynn Stone 16b; **Corbis** Adrian Arbib 15, /William
Gottlieb 13, /Earl & Nazima Kowall 18, /Brian Vikander
17t; **Ecoscene** Peter Cairns 16t; **FLPA** Ray Bird 8t,
/Nigel Cattlin 12, /Peter Dean 17b, /Mitsuaki Iwago 4;
Getty Images 14br, /Lisa Adams 6, /Gordon Clayton
8b, /Lester Lefkowitz 11, /Reneé Lynn 9, /James Martin
19, /Mecky FC, title page, /Tim Platt 14t; **Still Pictures**
Chlaus Lotscher 5

CONTENTS

Words in **bold** can be found in the Glossary on page 22.

Why we need cows

Do you know where milk comes from?
Or the shoes you wear on your feet?
Where do we get the meat to make tasty
beefburgers? All these things come from cows.

4

Cows working in the fields in Cuba.

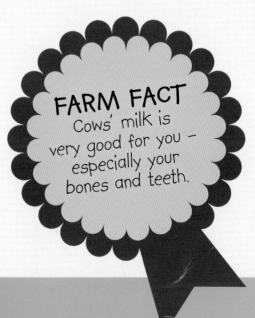

Cows are very important animals. They give us milk, leather and meat. In some countries, cows work in the fields. They pull **ploughs** to break up the soil. Then the farmer can plant crops such as **wheat** and **maize**.

5

Cows from nose to tail

Cows are big animals. A fully grown cow is about 1.5m tall and weighs around 600kg. That's the same as 30 six-year-old children!

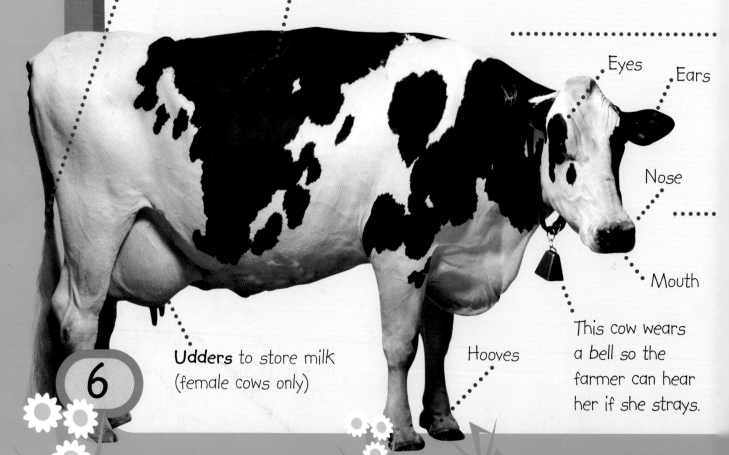

Tail to flick away flies

Thick skin covered in hair

Eyes

Ears

Nose

Mouth

This cow wears a bell so the farmer can hear her if she strays.

Hooves

Udders to store milk (female cows only)

FARM FACT
Cows use their long tongues to wrap around stems of grass and weeds and pull them out of the ground.

Height of cow

Height of six-year-old child

Each day a cow spends eight to ten hours just eating grass.

It's a cow's life...

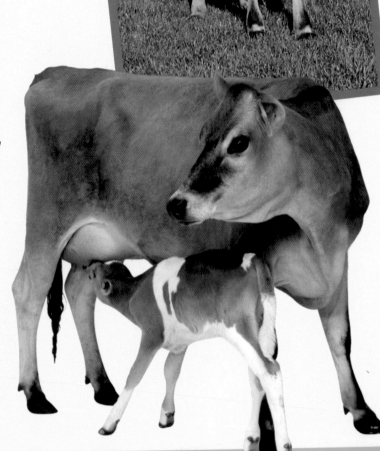

This cow has a baby cow, or **calf**, inside her. Before the baby is born, it has to grow inside its mother for nine months.

The first milk the mother feeds her calf is special. It helps the calf grow big and strong.

When the calf is about a week old, the farmer will start to feed it **pellets**.

At six months, the calf will eat grass in a field with other cows.

At about two years, the female calf can have a baby of its own.

Most cows live for about twelve years.

These baby calves are about ten weeks old.

9

Moo chew

A cow's stomach is very special.
Your stomach has only one main part,
but a cow's stomach has four!

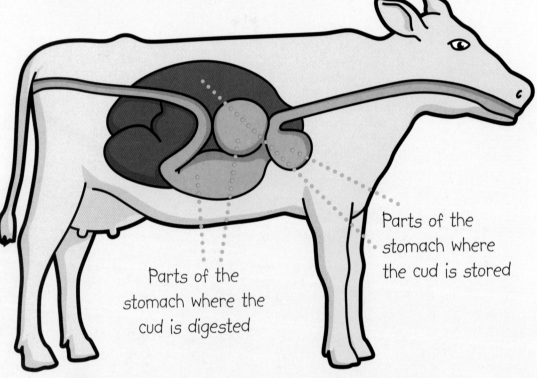

Parts of the
stomach where the
cud is digested

Parts of the
stomach where
the cud is stored

1 When a cow eats grass, it chews
it just enough to make it easy to swallow.
The partly chewed grass, or **cud**, is stored
in the first two parts of the cow's stomach.

FARM FACT
A cow's stomach can hold up to 227 litres of partly digested food. That's enough to fill a paddling pool!

2 When the first two parts of the cow's stomach are full, the cud comes up from the stomach to the cow's mouth to be chewed again.

3 After the cud has been chewed some more, it goes to the third and fourth parts of the cow's stomach, where it is **digested**. Some of this digested food goes to the udders, where it is made into milk.

From cow to carton

These cows are being milked by machine in a **milking parlour**. Using modern machines, farmers can milk more than 100 cows per hour. In some countries, farmers still milk their cows by hand.

A tanker takes the milk to a **dairy** where it is heated up until it is very hot to kill any germs. Once the milk has cooled down, it is safe to drink. The milk is then put into bottles or cartons, ready to go to the shops.

FARM FACT
Female cows cannot make milk until they have had a baby calf. Farmers milk each cow twice a day.

13

Why keep cows?

Not all cows are kept for milk. Many cows are kept for their meat. Meat from a cow is called beef.

The beef in beefburgers comes from cows.

The cow's skin can also be made into leather. Leather is used to make shoes, bags, belts and furniture.

Even cow **dung** has its uses. This African tribeswoman is using cow dung mixed with grass and twigs to build a hut. When the mixture is dry, it will be as strong as cement.

In Tibet, herdsmen build walls out of cow dung to protect their tents from the wind.

15

Cow cousins

Many different types of cow can be found all over the world.

HIGHLAND
These cows are from Scotland. They are famous for their long shaggy hair and curved horns.

TEXAS LONGHORN
These large cows with extra-long horns were brought to America by the Spanish over 500 years ago.

16

INDU-BRAZILIAN

These cows have the biggest ears of any type of cow. They live in hot countries such as Brazil.

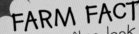

FARM FACT

Cows often look the same to us, but farmers are very good at recognizing them and often know them by name.

POLL HEREFORD

This is a very old type of British cow. The word 'polled' means hornless.

Cow customs

INDIA

In India, cows are **sacred** and must not be killed or hurt. Sacred cows are even allowed to wander through busy city streets full of traffic!

SWITZERLAND

Every year, Swiss people celebrate when the cows return to the mountain grasses. There are feasts with music and **yodelling** contests.

AFRICA

In many parts of Africa, cows are used instead of money. If a man from the Masai tribe wants to get married, it will cost him a lot of cows. He may have to give his bride's father 30 cows.

FARM FACT
In India and Nepal it is good luck to give a cow a snack, such as a piece of bread or fruit, to eat.

A Masai bride in traditional wedding costume.

19

Farmyard fun

Milk from cows is used to make butter, cheese, yoghurt and chocolate. You can make your own butter. Just follow these steps:

1 Pour the cream from some full-cream milk into a jam jar with a lid.

2 Screw the lid onto the jam jar. Make sure the lid is on tightly.

3 Shake the jam jar up and down.

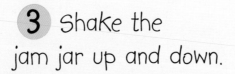

Warning to teachers and parents: Do not try this activity with children who have an intolerance to dairy products.

FARM FACT
It takes about 10 cups of milk to make 150g of butter – the amount you need to make a birthday cake!

4 Keep shaking...

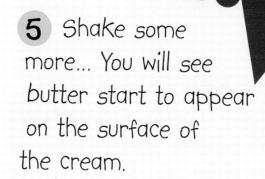

5 Shake some more... You will see butter start to appear on the surface of the cream.

6 When you have made enough butter, use a plastic knife to spread it onto a slice of bread. Some people like to add a little salt to their butter.

Glossary and Index

calf a baby cow

cud partly chewed grass which is stored in the cow's stomach and chewed again before being digested

dairy where milk is heated to kill germs and put into bottles or cartons

digested food which is broken down so that the body can use it for energy

dung cow's poo

fuel something that is burned to make heat or energy

maize type of corn or grain

milking parlour place where cows are milked

pellets small balls of food given to cows and other farm animals

plough farm machine used to break up soil and make fields ready for planting

sacred especially important or holy

udders part of a cow where milk is made and stored

wheat a plant grown for its grains, which are used to make flour

yodelling type of musical call used in Switzerland

23

Ideas for teachers and parents

- Make a poster to show how milk finds its way from the cow to the home. Ask the children to illustrate each stage in the process.

- Make a cow collage. Draw an outline of a cow on a large piece of paper. Have fun looking through magazines and newspapers and cutting out cow-related pictures. Look out for scraps of cow print material and any other odds and ends to liven up the children's pictures. Fill in the cow outline by sticking on the bits and pieces that you have collected.

- Research different breeds and make factsheets on the children's favourite breeds. Some cows look amazing!

- With the children, find out why milk is good for you. What does it contain? What parts of the body does it benefit?

- Challenge the children to think of stories, jokes and rhymes featuring cows, for example, 'Hey Diddle Diddle' and 'Jack and the Beanstalk'.

- See who can spot the most cows on a car, bus or train journey. Can you identify the breeds?

- If possible, visit a children's farm where children can see real live cows.

- Make a Highland cow mask. Cut eye-holes out of a paper plate and draw on a big cow nose. Add a woolly fringe and stick on ears and horns. Make holes on each side of the plate and add elastic so the mask can be worn.

- Make a simple wordsearch using cow-related vocabulary from this book.

- Visit **www.moomilk.com** for a fun and accessible website giving more information about the dairy industry and cows. **www.highlandtoffee.com** is a bright, activity-packed website about Toffee, the Highland cow. Children can read stories, colour in pictures on-screen and play a variety of games.

24

PLEASE NOTE
- Website information is correct at time of going to press. The publishers cannot accept liability for links or information found on third-party websites.
- The activity on pages 20–21 is not suitable for children with an intolerance to dairy products.